Better Homes and Gardens®

color
schemes
made easy

Meredith® Books
Des Moines, Iowa

color schemes made easy

Editor: Vicki L. Ingham

Contributing Project Manager/Writer: Shelley Stewart

Senior Associate Design Director: Doug Samuelson

Contributing Graphic Designers: Chad Johnston, Beth Runcie, Joe Wysong, Conyers Design, Inc.

Copy Chief: Terri Fredrickson

Publishing Operations Manager: Karen Schirm

Edit and Design Production Coordinator: Mary Lee Gavin

Book Production Managers: Pam Kvitne, Marjorie J. Schenkelberg, Rick von Holdt, Mark Weaver

Contributing Copy Editor: Jane Schorer Meisner

Contributing Proofreaders: Becky Etchen, Sherry Hames, Nancy Ruhling

Indexer: Sharon Duffy

Editorial Assistant: Kaye Chabot

Meredith® Books

Editor in Chief: Linda Raglan Cunningham

Design Director: Matt Strelecki

Managing Editor: Gregory H. Kayko

Executive Editor: Denise L. Caringer

Publisher: James D. Blume

Executive Director, Marketing: Jeffrey Myers

Executive Director, New Business Development: Todd M. Davis

Executive Director, Sales: Ken Zagor

Director, Operations: George A. Susral

Director, Production: Douglas M. Johnston

Business Director: Jim Leonard

Vice President and General Manager: Douglas J. Guendel

Better Homes and Gardens® Magazine

Editor in Chief: Karol DeWulf Nickell

Deputy Editor, Home Design: Oma Blaise Ford

Meredith Publishing Group

President, Publishing Group: Stephen M. Lacy

Vice President-Publishing Director: Bob Mate

Meredith Corporation

Chairman and Chief Executive Officer: William T. Kerr

In Memoriam: E. T. Meredith III (1933-2003)

Copyright © 2004 by Meredith Corporation, Des Moines, Iowa.
First Edition.
All rights reserved. Printed in the United States of America.
Library of Congress Control Number: 2004102153
ISBN: 0-696-22126-8

All of us at Meredith® Books are dedicated to providing you with information and ideas to enhance your home. We welcome your comments and suggestions. Write to us at: Meredith Books, Home Decorating and Design Editorial Department, 1716 Locust St., Des Moines, IA 50309-3023.

If you would like to purchase any of our home decorating and design, cooking, crafts, gardening, or home improvement books, check wherever quality books are sold. Or visit us at: bhgbooks.com.

For more information on the Rainbow Color Selector shown on page 13, visit www.eksuccess.com or www.k1c2.com. The color selector allows you to place the wheel over the fabric or paint you wish to match and find appropriate coordinating colors.

HOW TO USE
THIS BOOK

Are you ready to choose a color scheme? Wonderful—you're going to have fun. This idea book will help you simplify the subject of color. Here's some guidance on using the book.

The first chapter offers an overview of color and its emotional effects, complete with a short quiz to determine your personal color profile. Easy-to-understand color wheels and a glossary of terms help you understand how color works. Then comes an important part—suggestions for where to start.

Each chapter deals with one color and some of its shades. Large photos show rooms with beautiful color schemes, and the text explains why each combination works. Each room is accompanied by a color palette showing the hues in the scheme and their relative proportions. If you want to duplicate the scheme, you'll know how much of each color to use—lots of cream or just a little, a dash of red or a generous swath.

The last chapter answers frequently asked questions about color. As a bonus, the last 32 pages are your color-scheme sampler: All of the color palettes in the book are reproduced large-scale so you can cut out these pages and take them with you when you shop for fabric, paint, and accessories.

If you like a color scheme you see on the pages, the best way to re-create the scheme is to take the page with you when you shop. Match the printed colors to paint chips or ask someone at the paint store to scan the printed color to determine a matching paint color.

The possibilities are endless, and now you can surround yourself with colors that are right for you. This book makes it easy!

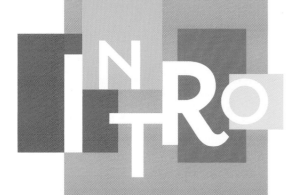

Table of Contents

The Joy of COLOR

The eye revels in color.
Whether it's a riotous rainbow of exuberant shades or as gentle as the first light of dawn, color invariably claims attention and can be considered one of life's great gifts.

There is a strong emotional component to color—it can make you feel happy, peaceful, or fully energized, even if you don't quite understand why. By learning how each color works, you can choose the right color schemes for the home that affects and reflects you and your family.

LIQUEUR CORDIAL-MEDOC

Color palette is on page 166.

THE EMOTIONAL LANGUAGE OF COLOR

When you decorate your home, you'll be much happier with the results if your color scheme carries the right emotional impact. Color is a powerful but intensely personal factor that can either bring forth the best in your natural temperament—or not. The colors that surround you on a daily basis can recharge your energy, help you relax, or deplete your ability to cope with stress. If everyone were alike, it would be easy to determine which hues produce a peaceful and productive state of mind. Unfortunately there isn't a pat formula for coming up with the perfect color scheme because each individual is different. Knowing the colors that affect you in a positive way is a good start.

A quick look at some of the qualities traditionally associated with the colors below may be helpful. Then, as an exercise in seeing how your personality relates to color, turn the page and take the quiz to find your color type.

To illustrate how color and emotions are inextricably linked, pair these descriptive words with the colors that often are associated with them:

◆ **BOLD**	◆ **PURPLE**
◆ **SNOBBISH**	◆ **GREEN**
◆ **ENVIOUS**	◆ **YELLOW**
◆ **MELANCHOLY**	◆ **RED**
◆ **CHEERFUL**	◆ **WHITE**
◆ **INNOCENT**	◆ **BLUE**

If you matched Bold Red, Snobbish Purple, Envious Green, Melancholy Blue, Cheerful Yellow, and Innocent White, then it shows you've absorbed some of the color associations typical of Western culture and literature.

RED This is an action color—bold, vigorous, energetic, stepping out in front. It can raise your blood pressure, stimulate your appetite, or even make you feel somewhat anxious or irritable. Burgundy, ruby, and maroon seem elegant, prosperous, and satisfied. Shades of pink promote a sense of well-being and happiness.

ORANGE Warm, friendly, and invigorating, orange is a color for which the shade dramatically affects its emotional impact. Pure orange often feels strident and discordant, but deeper tones of rust and terra-cotta or lighter tints of peach or salmon are restful and also flattering to most skin tones.

YELLOW Happy, joyous, uplifting yellow evokes the same feelings as a sunny day. Pure yellow is so bright that it may be hard to live with, but pale shades are expansive and wholesome and promote clear thinking. Deep yellow and golden tones are friendly and can seem either intimate or exotic, depending on the accent colors.

GREEN This is the color of rejuvenation, new growth, and fresh promise. It is also the color of restful reflection and wisdom. It has the ability to revive and also to soothe, but the particular shade is all-important—yellow-tone greens are more stimulating; blue-tone greens are more calming.

BLUE Small doses of primary or medium blue are homey and comforting, bringing down blood pressure and slowing the breathing rate. The same colors in large amounts can seem uncomfortably formal. Some shades of blue produce an icy chill, but those leaning toward red (periwinkle) or green (turquoise) are warmer and more welcoming.

PURPLE Creative, off-beat, and often surprising, purple ranges from meditative lavender, which is the color of dusk, to darkly sophisticated eggplant. In its pure form, purple is indisputably regal; in paler variations, it adds an element of lighthearted fun and restfulness.

NEUTRALS (BEIGE, TAUPE, BROWN, WHITE, GRAY, BLACK) Refreshing because they offer a quiet alternative to color, neutrals are also the peacemakers that separate brighter shades to help them get along. Pale tints are expansive and reasonable; darker tones are dramatic and graphic, even in small amounts.

WARM

WHAT'S YOUR COLOR TYPE?

Color is a little like magic—it affects your physical well-being, your activity level, and even your mood, all without your awareness that something outside you is changing your perception of reality.

Have you ever felt uncomfortable in a room but didn't know why? It probably wasn't the room's temperature or style of furniture that affected you. It's more likely that the color was too intense or seemed too cold and sterile. Or maybe it was because a barrage of different colors jangled your nerves, or an all-beige room was so boring that you couldn't find anything to interest you.

This is why it's so important to have as much self-knowledge as possible. The exercise on the opposite page will help you gain insight into how you relate to color.

NEUTRAL

COOL

Color palettes are on pages 169, 179, and 183.

This short inventory can be a great help, but there are no right or wrong answers. As you imagine yourself doing each activity, also think of a color you associate with it. Write that color in the space.

The possible color choices are Red, Pink, Orange, Yellow, Green, Blue, Purple, Brown, Beige, Taupe, Gray, Black, and White.

ACTIVITY	COLOR CHOICE
1. Going to bed	
2. Eating breakfast	
3. Lounging in your bathrobe	
4. Soaking in the tub	
5. Cooking a meal	
6. Fixing your hair	
7. Driving your car	
8. Picking flowers	
9. Harvesting your garden	
10. Listening to music	
11. Putting on a scarf or tie	
12. Setting the table	
13. Going to a formal dance	
14. Eating at your favorite restaurant	
15. Having a romantic dinner	
16. Putting up the patio umbrella	
17. Placing a wreath on the door	
18. Sitting with a refreshing drink	
19. Reading in front of the fire	
20. Potting indoor plants	
21. Dressing for work	
22. Taking a bike ride	
23. Swimming in a pool	
24. Entertaining good friends	
25. Boating on a river	
26. Meditating or daydreaming	
27. Cooking for the holidays	
28. Talking with your best friend	
29. Jogging after work	
30. Celebrating getting a job	
31. Hosting a wine tasting party	
32. Attending a wedding	
33. Arranging a bowl of fruit	
34. Discussing a favorite painting	

HOW DO YOU SCORE?

Find your color choices in the following basic categories—warm, cool, and neutral.

A—WARM COLORS:
Red, Pink, Orange, Yellow

B—COOL COLORS:
Green, Blue, Purple

C—NEUTRAL COLORS:
Brown, Beige, Taupe, Gray, Black, White

Next, assign an **A** to each of your warm colors, a **B** to each cool color, and a **C** to each neutral color. Count how many you listed in each category.

WARM		**A**s
COOL		**B**s
NEUTRAL		**C**s

Turn the page to see your Personal Color Profile.

Color palette is on page 189.

YOUR PERSONAL COLOR PROFILE

HOW DO YOU REACT TO COLOR?

- Mostly **A**s? You come alive with energizing colors. Use these in the active rooms of your home: entryways, hallways, dining rooms, rooms for entertaining, and playrooms. Enliven any neutral rooms with warm accent colors.
- Mostly **B**s? You respond to soothing colors. Use them in rooms for rest and relaxation, such as the bedroom, living room, home office, spa, or sunporch.
- Mostly **C**s? You like to keep your options open. Neutral colors are perfect for rooms that connect to other rooms, rooms that contain collections of art or objects, or rooms where you spend the most time, such as kitchens and bathrooms.
- Tie between two categories? Distribute the color "temperatures" throughout your home in doses compatible with the room's purpose. Bridge warm and cool colors with plenty of neutrals.

SUGGESTIONS:

- In the back of this book is a 32-page section with large color swatches of the color schemes that are featured. Cut out this section or take the book with you when choosing paint or fabrics.
- It's very helpful to use a color wheel when choosing compatible colors because the wheel graphically shows the relationships between different shades.

YOUR PERSONAL SPACE *If ever there is a place to surround yourself with colors that make you feel good, it's in your own home. Let the space fully reflect your personality.*

COLOR CHARACTERISTICS

WARM COLORS: Active colors that move forward, communicate vigor, cheer you, excite passions, stimulate appetite, promote conversation, and evoke emotions.

COOL COLORS: Passive colors that recede into the background, cool you down, calm your nerves, lift your spirits, promote introspection, and generally are soothing.

NEUTRAL COLORS: Open-minded colors that are easy on the eyes, symbolize a down-to-earth attitude, make you feel safe and secure, and work well with other colors.

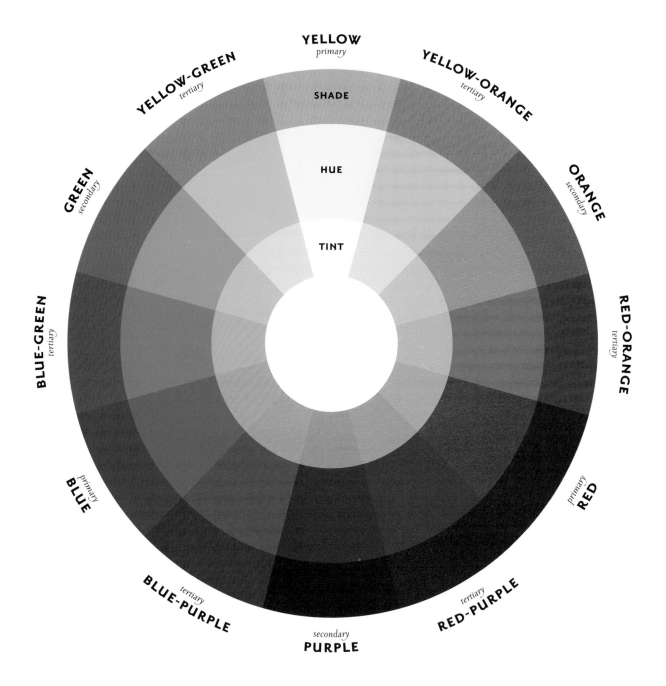

YELLOW *primary*

YELLOW-ORANGE *tertiary*

YELLOW-GREEN *tertiary*

ORANGE *secondary*

GREEN *secondary*

RED-ORANGE *tertiary*

BLUE-GREEN *tertiary*

RED *primary*

BLUE *primary*

RED-PURPLE *tertiary*

BLUE-PURPLE *tertiary*

PURPLE *secondary*

SHADE

HUE

TINT

COLOR BASICS

Even if you're familiar with a color wheel, it still may be something of a mystery. What do the sections of color mean? How do you use it? The wheel is nothing more than a simple way of showing how each color relates to other colors. It is a tool to help you choose pleasing combinations.

Color has its own vocabulary. Learning a few simple terms will help you understand how it works; then you can use it to best advantage when planning your color scheme.

The words **COLOR** and **HUE** are interchangeable. The **PRIMARY** colors—red, blue, and yellow—are the three basic colors from which all other colors are mixed. If you mix two primary colors together, the result is a **SECONDARY** color: For example, red + blue = violet, often called purple; blue + yellow = green; and yellow + red = orange. Purple, green, and orange are the secondary colors. Going further, mixing a primary color and a secondary color next to it forms a **TERTIARY** color. For example, blue + green = blue-green, which is a tertiary color.

Colors next to each other on the wheel are **ANALOGOUS** *(above right)*. Because they share a common component—yellow and green or green and blue, for instance—they always look good with each other. Opposites on the color wheel—red and green, orange and blue, or purple and yellow—are **COMPLEMENTARY** colors *(center right)*, and each makes the other look more intense.

A **SPLIT COMPLEMENTARY** color scheme is made up of one color plus the two colors that are analogous to its complement *(below right)*. For instance, one split complementary is the combination of green + red-purple + red-orange. This might be too intense in its pure form, but it is very attractive in lighter or darker shades.

When any three colors are equally spaced, they are called **TRIADS**; a color scheme composed of triads is balanced but somewhat overwhelming, so one of the colors needs to take precedence with the other two as accents.

Some colors are considered **WARM,** and some are **COOL.** Looking at the color wheel *opposite,* you'll see that half of the colors are warm, and half are cool. A warm color scheme may need a little cool to tone it down; likewise, you can enliven a cool color scheme with a bit of warm to keep it from going completely cold.

PURE hues are **SATURATED** hues, meaning that they are intense, undiluted color. The **INTENSITY** refers to the color's strength, while the **VALUE** is its lightness or darkness. Mixing pure hues with white creates light values called **TINTS**, while mixing them with black or other dark colors results in darker values called **TONES**. Mixing a hue with its complement softens and mutes the color. Slight differences in colors are called **SHADES**.

BALANCE is extremely important; try to choose colors of similar intensity. Pure hues, all warm colors, or all cool colors are unpleasant for most people, so the majority of workable color schemes have some combination of shades, tints, and tones.

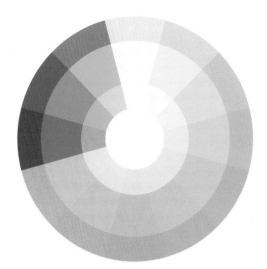

ANALOGOUS

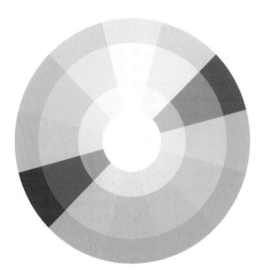

COMPLEMENTARY

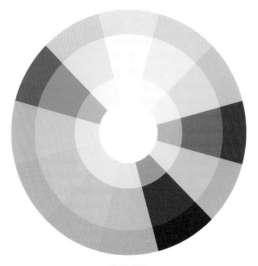

SPLIT COMPLEMENTARY

Color palette is on page 169.

STARTING POINT:
A FAVORITE COLOR

If a particular color always makes you feel good, then it might be the perfect beginning for an entire color scheme. When working around one color, establish a palette with your favorite hue as the main element and add white, off-white, and perhaps one or two harmonizing accent colors. Or to create a mainly monochromatic room, focus on one shade of your favorite color and add slight variations as accents.

When choosing secondary accents, one time-tested method is to combine warm with warm or cool with cool. If your objective is to temper the warmth or coolness of the room, choose accent colors from the other side of the color wheel.

Decorated in a rosy pink so rich that it verges on red, this bedroom has cream walls and multicolor cream, beige, and rose draperies to lighten the room and act as a soothing counterbalance to the vibrant pink. The pale blue-green loveseat repeats a bit of color found in the draperies; it's also a complementary color for pink.

TWO BIG FAMILIES *Colors can be classified as either warm or cool. If the color has yellow undertones, it is warm (orange, fire-engine red, yellow-green). If it has blue undertones, it is cool (royal blue, maroon, deep forest green). This principle also applies to lighter shades of the color—the warm pinks in this room, for example.*

STARTING POINT:
A CLASSIC COMBINATION

Despite brief color trends that come and go, certain combinations have proven to be perennial favorites. Although the in-vogue shades may vary from year to year, such standards as blue and yellow, blue and white, and the all-American red, white, and blue are as popular as ever. One of these may be a good choice for your room because such classic combinations never go out of style, they're easy to live with, and you'll always be able to find compatible accessories.

In this bedroom a color scheme of blue and white with touches of red, drawn from the hand-hooked flag wall hanging, creates a powerful setting for colonial-style furnishings. Despite the room's stark white walls (a fact of life in many rented spaces), there is abundant color in the vintage linens, all of which go together well because each is a variation of primary blue. White offers relief from so many medium-tone cool blues, while minor bits of bright red warm up the room and draw attention to accent pieces.

GROUP PIECES FOR IMPACT *Color is as good a starting point as any when accessorizing a room. A grouping of objects in the same one or two colors, displayed together, acquires the status of a collection and is a more important decorative element than those same objects displayed separately.*

Color palette is on page 177.

Color palette is on page 162.

ONE STEP AWAY *You can use more than one fabric pattern in a room, but for cohesiveness, each should have one or more colors in common with the primary fabric. For instance, a room might draw its color scheme from an upholstery fabric with blue and green on a cream background. One accent pillow might be blue, another blue and green, and another green and cream.*

STARTING POINT:
DRAW COLOR FROM FABRIC

One of the easier ways to choose a color scheme is to copy the color combination in a favorite fabric. Textiles, after all, are designed by professionals who are knowledgeable about color. If you like the fabric, you'll probably feel comfortable in a room decorated from the same palette even if you use the colors in different proportions.

The colors in this cheerful family room come from the lighthearted fabric on the sofa. Various stripes in the screen-printed cotton inspire sunny yellow walls and pillows, upbeat red-plaid and spring-green chairs, and a periwinkle bench. Over the windows a second printed fabric harmonizes because it contains the same yellow, red, and green as the sofa—this time on a white background that draws the white-painted woodwork into the mix. Don't worry if some of the smaller accents are minor variations on the basic color scheme—these keep your room from appearing contrived.

ONE ROOM—THREE LOOKS

Having settled upon a color scheme, you still need to determine how much of each color to use and where to use it. This step is as important as picking the colors. These rooms are identical except for walls painted in three colors pulled from the sofa fabric. This one change makes a big difference!

The mocha room *below* is somewhat formal and is especially elegant at night when lamplight illuminates the corner and other walls go dark. Straw-color walls, *opposite above*, reflect daylight and provide a neutral background that goes well with almost anything, an important factor to consider if you often rotate accessories. Rosy pink walls and matching draperies, *opposite below*, surround the furniture in a monochromatic embrace of color, adding a designer-like quality to the room.

FINDING BALANCE *Color proportions make an enormous difference in how a room looks and feels. The vivid color you use as an accent may seem overwhelming on larger surfaces such as walls or carpeting. Or you might find that you appreciate its powerful statement. There's no right or wrong way to allocate various colors—it's a matter of preference.*

Color palettes are
on page 170.

ART-DIRECTED ELEMENTS *Emphasize even a small painting or sculpture by displaying it against an accent wall of a different color. The art becomes more of a focal point, and colors in the room work to support it.*

STARTING POINT:
ART

Dramatic art inspires dramatic rooms—a painting of flowers can grow into a garden-style room or a one-tone line drawing can give rise to a sophisticated room in neutrals. As every collector knows, art's appeal is an extremely personal thing, and a favorite piece can be the jumping-off point for a color scheme that reflects a vital part of yourself.

This expressive room draws from colors in the painting, a bold abstract of blues and greens. Accent walls painted in these saturated hues almost seem to be extensions of the artwork. The illusion continues with more of the colors in the rug and curvilinear seating. Notice how spiky daffodils echo the tiny bit of yellow in the painting, bringing life and warmth to the cool-tone room.

Color palette is on page 180.

Color palette is on page 162.

STARTING POINT:
A FAVORITE OBJECT

Collectors take note: That pottery plate or antique lamp you're so fond of can inspire the color for your whole room. When you fashion a color scheme around any favorite object, that object immediately seems more important because the space becomes a made-to-order showcase.

A love of old-world blue and white pottery was the inspiration for this harmonious color scheme of blue, white, and fresh yellow. The large tureen on the table started it all—but cheerful yellow walls and draperies team with the cool blue and white to add spark to the mix.

You'll notice that elements in both rooms take their color cues from the pottery. Napkins and blue-trimmed chairs in the dining room, as well as pillows, lamps, and draperies in the adjoining living room, are close in tone so they go together very well.

PULLED TOGETHER *Bind rooms with a thread of color that leads the eye from one area to another. For example, if the dining room has yellow walls, repeat the yellow in the living room—even a bowl of apples can do the job. Yellow-print pillows or draperies would make the connection even more explicit.*

YELLOW

Bursting onto the scene with the unapologetic zest of freshly squeezed lemon, exuberant yellow stimulates even a bland color scheme with its lively freshness. Choose vibrant yellow in shades from palest buttercream to savory mustard or complex curry. As the main color or as a garnish for other hues, it creates a piquant blend.

SUCCESSFUL COMBINATION Two complementary colors, opposites on the color wheel, look best when they are roughly equal in intensity and value: Use pale with pale and deep with deep.

f you're faced with a boxy room that has no interesting features, harness the power of color to create a focal point. In this living room, harlequin-inspired panels of citron yellow and cream silk become a much-needed focal point that frames and adds emphasis to a small but important painting. On the adjoining wall, more yellow silk cascades down the windows in a waterfall of fabric.

Why is this high-style treatment so effective? Again it's because of color—complementary color. The walls are a very dark and elegant shade of aubergine (eggplant). Since purple is the complement of yellow, the aubergine and citron yellow follow the same principle; each makes the other look more vivid, bringing out the best in both. Behind the bright panels, the aubergine walls are such a dark shade that they almost seem to disappear in low light, giving the illusion of a much more spacious room. Rather than adding more color to the mix, the pale gold loveseat and rug quietly echo the robust yellow silk.

A FAMILY RESEMBLANCE While drawing inspiration from a fabric, paint and accessories are free to depart from the exact shades, as long as they are the same basic hue.

Does your heart leap with pleasure when you walk in the garden on a sunny day? You can get almost the same feeling from a color scheme. This sunshine yellow bedroom does its best to duplicate a garden with fresh colors, outdoor materials, and floral motifs. Along with yellow, white, and natural wood, there are myriad shades of leaf green, rosebud pink, and violet. As in nature, the beauty of the whole is composed of countless colors, which can vary immensely although they're only a few shades apart.

How do you select compatible colors for a multicolor scheme? This one starts with the bedspread fabric that sets the mood with bright blossoms, trailing vines, and yellow trimming; the fabric inspires furniture and accessories in slight variations of its principal colors.

Sunny yellow walls and a pale floor infuse the room with reflected light. The trim, shutters, and garden-style furniture are white, which helps to unify the room and adds to the outdoorsy feeling.

Sophisticated in blonde and black, the restrained palette in this living room lets art and artifacts take precedence over color. But wouldn't light colors show the pieces off even better? Here's the reason for so much black and dark wood: They add weightiness and drama because all-pale tints would be too bland for the exotic carvings and artwork.

What else is happening to draw attention to the art? Line, color, and architecture play a part. The black leather daybed adds a strong horizontal element repeated by black shelves, forcing the eye to sweep the room and take everything in. Simple upholstery repeats the tone of the floor, a broad expanse uncompromised by rugs. Color-blocked recesses in different shades accent especially important sculptures.

Subtle accessories and flowers, in a paprika red color drawn from the painting, enliven the room and keep it from looking like an art museum.

REPETITION, REPETITION In design, the word "cohesion" refers to a room that is pulled together well. Any room can be more cohesive if you select a few key elements—color, shape, line, or material—and repeat them several times for emphasis.

FOR MAXIMUM EMPHASIS Use contrasting colors to draw attention to furnishings. Display dark against light or bright or conversely, light or bright against dark.

This room is proof that vibrant color can coexist happily with classically elegant furnishings. In their day, period furnishings were often used with very bright colors. So revive the practice by using a vibrant contemporary color for walls while keeping the antiques you have. Furniture and accessories may look even richer in contrast.

Although rarely used in today's formal interiors, gold and black is a color combination often found in nature, where the contrast usually draws attention to the brighter shade. In this room the walls and even the draperies are gold—against this bright but still monochromatic background, the eye, for a change, is drawn to the darker furnishings.

You may have noticed that designers often use black to add sophistication and formality to a room. You can do the same thing. Just an accent here and there, and black works its magic. Inspired by marvelous faux-marble woodwork, black repeats in several other places. Black and white check upholstery also updates the chairs.

Guest rooms offer a wonderful chance to throw yourself into color wholeheartedly, experiment with offbeat combinations, and try some things you might not do in rooms that are used more often. This is the place for creative projects too. Instead of using the room as a repository for mismatched furniture, paint the furniture to go together or sew one glorious quilt from odds and ends of fabric. Houseguests will love the fact that you've put so much of yourself in the room, and you'll have lots of fun.

In this room, white is an essential calming element because everything else is color and movement. Pastels leap from the quilt to the furniture and even the walls, where color-blocked sections form a dynamic background. There are yellow, green, purple, and blue, but wait—no pink? Instead of too-predictable pink, there's an unexpected pink-tinted beige that keeps the room from sliding into the same-old-pastel color scheme.

GROUP VALUES When combining a number of different colors, use those with similar intensities and values. Anything too much darker or lighter immediately stands out.

You can create an exciting, almost foolproof room makeover without buying anything but paint. How? Choose fabric or an accessory already in your room and draw one or two accent colors from it. Then update tired walls—and maybe the ceiling too—by painting them in these new colors.

Each of these rooms has a yellow and green color scheme, but see what a difference the shade and intensity make. The breakfast room *below* has the colonial style furniture usually teamed with muted Americana colors, yet it easily adapts to upbeat shades pulled from the fabric—going so far as to have lemon yellow walls and a green ceiling. In the room *opposite* Majolica pottery inspires a gentle palette of soft yellow and green emboldened by touches of black.

SIMPLE ADJUSTMENTS Even if you decide to stick with the color scheme you have, you can vary the shades and proportions. Slight changes can rebalance a color scheme to produce a different effect.

ORANGE

The yummy orange has lent its name to a whole range of hues, skipping like a color gourmet from palest fruit-tone apricot and peach to melon, carrot, and pumpkin, pausing at earthy terra-cotta and ending at deepest rust. Like the orange, these warm colors are packed with energy, and they provide a good addition to cooler shades.

O ften the purest form of a color is too intense to be a main part of the color scheme. This is when you use the color but shift it toward darker or lighter shades. Imagine, for instance, how bright orange would have looked in this attic bedroom with its antique furniture, handwoven fabrics, and tribal rugs. It would have been far too jarring. Muted shades of terra-cotta are more appropriate. They lose a bit of orange's sharp edge but none of its warmth or decorative appeal.

Walls and ceiling are the first commitments in any room—most of these are a creamy white that seems to expand the space. Two accent walls have a gray-green sponged finish for definition (and are easily repainted if the room is changed). The terra-cotta bedspread, paler than the rug and pillows, is a lively note that works well with both the green walls and the yellow-pine furniture. Notice that the trunk is antique blue, the complement of terra-cotta. Like two old and dear friends, each color brings out the best in the other.

CONSIDER THE NATURAL LIGHT Abundant sunshine reflecting from the off-white walls offers relief from so many grayed colors. In rooms without so much light, you can go a little brighter with colors and get the same subdued effect.

DUAL FUNCTIONS Choose a piece of art because something in you responds to it, but don't overlook the effect that its subject and colors have on the room. It is far wiser to use art you love as the inspiration for a great room than to choose a bland or even boring piece just because it "goes."

Flattering to guests as few other colors are, this ripe-melon shade on the walls is a convivial backdrop for elegant gatherings. Anchored by woodwork in black faux marble, the melon walls are bright enough to reflect light from large windows in the daytime. At night when the draperies are drawn, the walls form a warm cocoon of color that has the effect of glowing firelight.

Then why doesn't the room seem overly warm? It's because of all the neutrals that cool it down. Taupe and a gold so pale it's almost cream cover most of the seating and the floor to keep the vivid room from overwhelming its occupants. Subdued patterns in the rug, pillows, and one chair repeat variations of the orange tone to harmonize with the walls (it's always a good idea to have paint or fabric samples with you when shopping to avoid costly mistakes).

The choice of art is interesting—notice how the large unframed painting deliberately draws the eye beyond the confines of the room to create a sense of more space. Its olive and brown colors, while not analogous to the melon walls, have the same warm yellow undertones, ensuring that they go together well.

rbane as only a loft can be, this room draws its color scheme in part from an exposed brick wall in various tones of deep orange, brown, and putty. The texture is all the more obvious in contrast to luxurious silk pillows that repeat its colors for a sophisticated blend of rough and rich.

How do you decide on a color scheme if you're coping with a permanent feature such as brick with many different tones? First, decide if you like the feature. If you don't, then paint it. If you do, then look for an accessory that contains the dominant colors, plus more!

The area rug pulls together the colors of the wall and ceiling and also contains eggplant. The bedspread picks up this color but leans slightly toward blue, the color that best complements orange tones. The other walls, although dramatic in shape, are basic white, and the floor is neutral polished concrete.

HEIGHTEN THE EFFECT When a favorite accessory, such as a patterned rug, has numerous different shades, pull out one or two and use them liberally in the room.

OPPOSITES ATTRACT Even if one is light and one is dark, complementary colors enhance each other. Bring in at least one touch of a color's complement to make your room seem more lively.

Blue and orange complement each other to perfection in a dining area influenced by Provence, a region of France. Floor-to-ceiling windows, framed by pinkish-orange Saltillo tiles cut to look like stone, flood the room with sunshine and make an ideal backdrop for the linens (in complementary blue and analogous yellow, of course!) that add such a punch of color.

Imagine how this room would look without the boldness of this intense blue and yellow. Sunflower yellow, a color beloved by the artist Van Gogh when he painted in Provence, appears prominently in the fabric. Strong orange and yellow in the place settings also keep the bright blue in check.

More Saltillo tile anchors the room with a sweep of pale orange on the floor. Light walls, hand-rubbed with glaze for an aged appearance, are an almost neutral balance for so much sunlit color, but wood tones and black-iron accents add the darker elements so necessary for depth.

PALE BUT STRONG If your color scheme is composed of such light tints that it seems to lack energy, add one or two slightly stronger elements of pattern or color. This works especially well when you add the complementary color of the tint.

Is a house with only pale tints doomed to be dull? No, not if you liven it up with brighter accents and pattern. Whether in small doses or amounts large enough to be dramatic, these dynamic elements will save your rooms from the too-pale blahs.

This apricot dining room has walls so faint that they're only a whisper of orange, yet it's remarkable how much color, personality, and sense of movement there is. Attracting immediate attention, the rug has a strong pattern of trailing green vines and leaves that grounds the room. Everything interesting shouldn't be at one level though, particularly if it's underfoot.

This room has interest at every level. A well-dressed table adds more color and pattern to keep the walls from seeming bland in comparison to the eye-catching rug. Placed atop a floor-length white tablecloth, another cloth in apricot, rose, and white plaid pulls the eye toward green dishes that repeat the leafy motif of the rug. Two chests delicately painted to resemble red-orange toile add more pattern and color to the mix.

Color and pattern aren't the only elements at work here. A peeling window frames a mirror that lures the eye with its reflections and, along with the rug, promotes the feeling of being in a garden.

Two rooms—one a charming bath and the other a sleek living room—have walls in roughly the same shade of peach. What makes them so different? It's how they do—or don't—combine pattern with color.

Nearly every surface in the bath *left* has pattern: The wallpaper, fabric, planter, and even the artwork have details to occupy the eye. Lots of white in fixtures and the ceiling balances the bright color and abundant pattern in the small room.

Now for the living room *opposite*—except for peach walls and a matching ceiling, it has neutral shades on every surface, and there's almost no pattern. Golden brown squares in pillows and the rug are the only color accents except for lush green plants. Living plants always bring out color and make a room seem more inviting.

TINTS AT THE TOP Keep the height of a ceiling in mind when choosing its color. Those high enough not to feel oppressive can benefit from color to match or contrast with walls, but those lower than 9 feet might need the expansive lift of white.

RED

Surrounded by more shy shades, red is the color that waves its hand wildly and begs to be noticed. Bolder and more energetic than most other colors, it is rarely reticent, making itself known in a strong clear voice that can't be ignored. Rosy as an apple, burnished into jewel tones, or stretched into pink by an infusion of white, there's a dynamic shade of red for every room.

Perhaps you've been afraid to indulge in really bright color (even though you love it) because its overwhelming intensity might get out of hand. You even may have found yourself sticking to neutral whites instead, to be safe. Well, relax a little and take a look at this very livable room furnished completely in white—and red.

A sprinkling of spicy red accents rescues this art-focused room from the blandness of too little color. The art, botanical drawings matted in white, shares the antique tones of muted flowers and olive-tone leaves on a parchment ground. Strong red, a vivid complement to the tiny amount of green in the drawings and a living plant, actually draws more attention to this low-key art because it frames several pieces for emphasis.

Despite its strength, you can see that the red is used with tremendous discipline to lead the eye toward every level of the room. A tall folding screen that displays art is a dominant element, but more traditional frames at the other side balance its bright color. As the biggest block of red, the table base lends visual weight to the bottom of the room. Interesting throw pillows, piping on the slipcovers, and tall candles add the same color interest at a higher level.

o you have to choose between using either a bright color or a pronounced pattern? Absolutely not. You may feel exhilarated in a roomful of pattern, or you may feel that too much is simply too much. Whichever camp you're in, you can have the color and the pattern you love.

These two rooms make use of red and white toile, but one dives into the world of pattern wholeheartedly while the other is more restrained (if any room in bright red can be considered restrained). Both mix the toile with checked fabric and large amounts of white, but the proportion of pattern to solid color is quite different.

In the room *opposite*, only the deep tan floor is without pattern; other surfaces are in six different patterns with very similar reds. Another room *below* actually has more patterns, but they appear in much smaller doses against rosy red walls and neutral white bedding for a simpler, less cluttered appearance. Notice, too, that both of these rooms in red also have dashes of green, the complementary color.

KNOW THYSELF If you're not sure about your tolerance for definitive pattern combined with bright color, start small. Begin with patterned pillows or a border on draperies. Hold off on expensive, more permanent items such as wallpaper until you've discovered your limits.

I f you have a major piece of art, use it as a guide to painting your room to make the most of it. This room in near-primary colors shows how effective this approach can be. In spite of all the color, art is definitely the focal point.

Here, in fact, the mainly blue and green canvas is doubly emphasized because the surrounding wall is vibrant red—in effect becoming one large frame in a complementary color that rivets attention on the painting.

Now look at the color of the painting. The main colors are two shades of blue-green (analogous colors), and that blue-green has yellow undertones. To harmonize, all of the other colors in the room also contain yellow undertones. The red is a red-orange, the white is on the creamy side, and other walls and the ceiling are each a slightly different color of yellow. All of this ensures that the room is lively and that every color goes well together.

Wood and rattan furniture in natural tones offers relief from so much bright color. On the floor an Oriental rug in red with black and navy adds visual weight to anchor the room.

ARTFUL ADDITIONS To attract more attention to your favorite piece of art, draw out one of its stronger colors to use as a major accent. Paint at least one wall, line the backs of bookcases with fabric, or use piles of pillows in that hue.

Although delicate in comparison to its more robust cousins, pink is part of the red family and lives by the same house rules. Green is pink's complement; and black, white, and other neutrals are especially good accents. Because it is a warm color, pink goes well with other hues on the warm side of the color wheel, including yellow and other reds.

A genteel background, provided by shell pink walls, enables antique prints and a Majolica pottery collection to get the attention they deserve. A multicolor carpet in tones of rose, pale blue, black, and cream is dark enough to go with mahogany and black tole but light enough to echo the neutral upholstery. Woodwork, including the broad mantel and wide dentil molding around the ceiling, is traditional white to keep it from seeming overly heavy against the light pink.

Is this pink room so pale that it has no substance? Hardly. Dark furniture gives it visual weight, and nudges from such unexpected elements as a rich paisley lap robe, yellow roses, and animal-print cushions push the room into more adventurous color territory.

THE PROPER SETTING Create an atmosphere of luxury in your rooms by opting for a jewel-tone color scheme and polished surfaces. The exact color of the walls doesn't matter as long as it is dark and rich.

Here's a new twist on faux-painted wall treatments: In a departure from vertical stripes, these elegant striated walls have broad horizontal bands in two jewel-like shades of red—garnet and ruby. Dark stripes painted over the lighter red wall in a layered effect increase the apparent size of the room. Another strong horizontal line in the white crown molding is a contrast for the dark tones.

When the walls are so rich, it's important that other colors be intense enough to hold their own. To complement the red tones, slubbed silk chairs are peridot green, a yellow-green shade that is found again in the hydrangea and lime centerpiece. The ceiling is a deep gold, another warm color that adds an element of luxury. The rug has checks of cream and the same deep gold, playing off the angular lines on the walls.

Which accessories are appropriate in such a boldly elegant room? Only strong shapes with reflective surfaces—dark polished wood, sparkling silver, and Venetian glass and mirrors—do it justice.

In this richly tasteful living room, deep-seated comfort meets designer detail. The mottled leather-look walls are a tasteful combination of paprika red and chili brown, colors picked up from the classic handwoven rug. The walls, the rug, and cordovan furniture are roughly the same shade, and all of them are based on red.

With this much dark color predominating, how can this room still look so warm and inviting? One reason is that there's plenty of light, amplified by reflection from the high white ceiling.

Red-orange pillows and striped draperies in a print of orange, gold, and sage green also add color excitement to spice up the blend. The analogous accent colors relate to the red by sharing its warm yellow undertones, and sage green is the slightly subdued complement that enables the red to look its best.

CHOOSING SIDES Keeping a room on its toes requires a color scheme based on skillful combinations of light and dark, light and bright, bright and dark, or complementary colors. Look at the colors you've selected in all types of light before definitely deciding.

PURPLE

Lilac, larkspur, violet, plum, blackberry, wild grape, and orchid—like the plants from which they draw their names, these shades of purple explode on the senses in sweet bursts of color. Purple ranges from pale meditative lavender to a brilliant violet aura that electrifies a color scheme. The energy-charged intensity of bright violet or magenta may be too much to handle except in small amounts, but purple's more easy-going offshoots make charming long-term companions.

THE HOME AS GALLERY Deep-tone walls are an elegant backdrop for bright art you want to feature. To keep the room from seeming oppressively dark, use a pale carpet and plenty of well-directed lighting.

With exposed ductwork and concrete columns, lofts and remodeled buildings run the risk of looking coldly industrial, but powerful color transforms them into dramatic living spaces. In this bedroom neutral gray concrete teams with deep purple walls as dark as a desert sky, and then the walls burst into unexpected bloom with bright abstract paintings.

There are yellow, red, blue, and brown accents—all bright against the purple—so why does yellow look by far the strongest? It's because yellow is the complement of purple; against the dark purple walls it looks more vivid than any other color.

Moldings in this room are nothing special, so most of them are "painted out" to become almost invisible against walls of the same color. Bright white molding draws attention to one door only, identifying it as the way out and guiding the eye to the adjoining room.

Surrounded by orchid walls and tropical flowers, you might find it hard to believe you're at work instead of relaxing on an island. With walls and the vaulted ceiling painted in the same glowing tone, a cocoon of color surrounds you in the executive chair. A palette of bright pastels and soft greens comes from the Balinese screen. It's definitely not the corporate look, but who cares? In a home office, individuality and off-beat colors are appropriate.

Creative thought comes quite naturally in such a setting. The lack of a real desk, for instance, poses no problem. A painted-plywood tabletop rests on file cabinets hidden by fabric combining all the room's colors in its stripes. Weathered green chairs and a rustic side table take the place of more traditional seating for guests.

Sunlight streams through large windows trimmed with woodwork of ochre, green, and periwinkle and covered only by simple white blinds. The ceiling has skylights and exposed beams, painted taupe, to create an expansive feeling overhead.

COMMITTEE OF ONE Go for the colors you love, no matter how "unbusinesslike," when decorating your home office. You may feel more eager to tackle the day's work when you're comfortable in your surroundings.

74

I t's the playful interaction of high and low, white and bright, vertical and horizontal, and old and new that keeps this room upbeat. Add reflections on several planes with mercury glass and mirrored furniture, and the room is even more interesting.

Have you always assumed that vintage furnishings call for vintage colors? Not true. Combining the best of old and new, this bedroom has an up-to-the-minute color scheme of cool lavender and white with contemporary-looking accents of sharp acid green—a color that comes from antique vases. Warm yellow-green is close enough to yellow, lavender's complement, for it to have strong impact, but cool, silvery accents keep it in check.

What else is contemporary? Stylish curtains in two shades of lavender lift the eye, following the lead of thin silver stripes on the wall. A tufted bench and a subtly patterned rug ground the room with more soft lavender, and stacks of pillows in white, green, and cocoa add visual weight to the all-white bed.

ADD THE SEASONING To keep your pastel room from seeming too tame, throw in a bold color accent that's one step away from the complementary color. Instead of pure yellow with this lavender, for instance, the accent is yellow-green. Another good choice would be yellow-orange.

ROOM FOR EXTROVERTS Enliven a room by using one strong color plus its analogous and complementary colors as accents—the color scheme will seem vivacious and exciting. To keep the main color from overpowering the others, make sure they are all equally intense.

To create a setting where guests feel good and sparkling conversation flows, choose warm, convivial colors for the furnishings. In a bold display of saturated color against silvered walls, this dining room is resplendent.

What is the secret of its style? It's the confident mix of rich color and sumptuous fabric: purple silk draperies, warm paisley in British red, orange, and brown, and golden silk cushions to complement the purple. Alone each tone and texture is strong, but combine them, and they're magnificent!

With jewel-like warm colors making such an impact in soft furnishings, it's important that there's a cool-tone background for contrast. Walls have a metallic silver-leaf finish, and the floors are gleaming, diamond-stenciled wood. Old-world gold and black "marble" accents are impressive, but the proud center of attention is the light fixture in purple amethyst-glass, around which every other color revolves.

EASE INTO COLOR As with bold pattern, very bright color can be hard to live with. Test your tolerance on surfaces that can be repainted. Be wary of installing colorful but expensive fixtures that you may tire of before they wear out.

Y ou may be artistic, or a little quirky, or maybe you thrive on stimulating colors—whatever it is, you've probably considered an unconventional scheme for part of your home. Try bright choices in action areas: Playrooms, family rooms, kids' rooms, and kitchens usually are more lively than an adult bedroom, but if you can tolerate color "noise," any room will do.

Although one is in an older house and one is newly built, these two kitchens have a lot in common: Each has purple cabinets and other strong accents. The newer kitchen *below* has the latest in surfaces and convenience, yet the big news is its color scheme:

Purple and bright green cabinets send a shock wave that rocks the room. A wooden ceiling and generous amounts of white in the flooring and backsplash relieve the large chunks of color.

The older kitchen *above* has a fairly basic layout. So what's a creative soul to do? Use color and originality to make up for its shortcomings, teaming deep eggplant cabinets with walls covered in orange-painted paper that has been torn into pieces and applied like wallpaper. More handmade art papers in various colors and textures cover space beneath the cabinets and above the window.

NEVER SAY NEVER If you're not fond of a certain color, check out the latest shades and combinations before you abandon the idea completely—you may like them!

Do you like dark or light? If it's chocolate, you probably have your favorite. With color, too, some prefer dark and some prefer light, but purple aficionados can take their pick of many shades. Ranging from deepest eggplant to palest lilac, purple hues add either warmth or coolness to a room, depending on how much they lean toward red or blue. And chocolate brown, surprisingly, is a good tone to mix with almost any purple shade.

Deep purple transforms a bungalow living room *above* into an exceptionally stylish space, an elegant background for art and light-color furniture. Painting the walls and brick fireplace dusty purple unifies the room, camouflaging problem areas on the plaster walls as well. Wide moldings and windows are refreshingly white, but the oak floor is a deep gold complement to the dark walls. To pull it all together, a plaid fabric combines shades of eggplant, white, gold, and chocolate.

The lighter sitting room *below* is a lavender tint, made by blending pure purple with white. Although more reflective than darker tones, this pale shade is cool and restful even in bright daylight. Various shades of lavender, large amounts of white, and chocolate brown work together in a surprisingly sophisticated scheme, warmed and softened by the café au lait-color wainscot effect on the walls.

Mother Nature loves this color.

In azure skies and aquamarine water, in achingly blue hyacinths and forget-me-nots, or in deep underground caches of lapis and sapphire, she distributes these exquisite shades with a generous hand. Small wonder that blue has been a color scheme favorite for thousands of years. Styles may change, but tasteful blue is timeless.

SHIPSHAPE COMBINATION To maintain order in a small cabin, run a tight ship on color. Choose one color to feature in fabric and furniture, and make everything else white.

With an intense color such as bright blue, it helps to lighten the mood with shades of white (or other neutrals). In a paradoxical turn, the more white you use, the more vivid the color appears—you can appreciate the shade more when it's seen in the context of "negative" color. This applies not only to blue but also to any bold color.

Marine blue and crisp white trim echo the tones of sea and surf in this nautical room with a classic color scheme. Against the clean backdrop of white board-and-batten walls, clear blue fabrics in solids, patterns, and stripes stand out in contrast. Minimal color intrudes on this simple combination but natural wood, textured wicker, and louvered shutters add interest in its place.

C an the drumbeats of faraway lands be heard in homes with standard architecture? Yes, your rooms can reflect any culture because color has no nationality. Through the portal of purple walls, a clear blue dining room becomes a grotto-like setting that is as much a showcase for primitive art as it is a place to eat. With chairs covered in Guatemalan textiles and a handwoven rug underfoot, the room comes alive with vivid patterns. As dramatic as it is, the palette is simply an analogous color scheme of equally intense blue, purple, and red.

The wine red floor is a shade that bridges the red and purple, just as the purple is a bridge between red and blue. Against such saturated tones, even accent colors must be intense to have much impact. Bright yellow, green, red, and orange announce their presence in strong voices—with exotic accents.

CLOSE RELATIVES Any analogous (adjoining) colors create bold effects when used together: Try using cool blue, green, and yellow—or purple, fiery red, and orange. Deepen the tones or combine analogous pale tints for milder (and perhaps more livable) versions of analogous color schemes.

nless they have the balance of darker elements, all-pastel rooms run the risk of seeming too pale and lacking in drama. This exquisite living room includes dark wood, and despite the restraint of the color scheme, the overall effect is powerful. The blue and cream palette is set by porcelain vases, arrayed on the mantel like proud beauties surveying their effect on the room below.

All of the color and even the dainty blue patterns, separated by calming off-white and yellow upholstery, come from these vases. You'll notice that while the shades aren't identical, they are close enough to be compatible.

Much like a natural beauty, even a room with grace and refinement might become tiresome if it didn't also have an interesting personality. Dark wood moldings and an arresting painting give hints of a deeper character, and elements of yellow-green add a playful touch.

The dilemma in choosing colors for a baby's room is that the room should be ready before the baby is born. Pink or blue? Or yellow, to be safe? Why settle on one color? A multicolor scheme of bright pastels will suit your baby just fine and can adapt to suit an older sibling too.

Do you remember when you were a child? Blue skies made every day an adventure! These sky blue walls dotted with stars are no exception. Lower walls of pale yellow and blue stripes draw attention to the above-eye-level shelf, where decorative household items share space with baby's first toys.

Mismatched furniture painted in various pastels takes on a custom appearance with blue, lavender, pink, yellow, and green vying for attention. Neutral white keeps everything under control. Here's an observation: Even in this undeniably youthful "blue-sky" room, darker touches like wood flooring are needed to bring it down to earth.

Denim blue, rusty red, and warm white team up in a traditional, true-blue country-style color scheme. The color here comes from the fabrics and accessories rather than the walls. Set your theme with the bedding—it's the largest expanse of color. Choose curtains, quilts, and blankets to supply contrasting colors and accents.

Notice the wooden-spool cabinet—its color repeats the red in several patterns, condensing it into one bright spot of vivid red to become the main focal point (and the logical place to display prized Native American artifacts).

What else adds warmth to this mountain-style room with white walls? Natural wood is the key element. Wooden panels behind the bed are especially important because they provide a neutral backdrop for the multicolor rugs hung over the headboard.

INSTANT AGE To create a sense of warmth in a room with vintage furnishings, mix colorful patterns with abandon. As long as they have at least one color in common, they'll go together but will look as if they've been gathered over the years.

SETTING THE TONE Keep a steady hand when doling out color in a color-plus-white room because the total amount adds up. No matter what the color, the effect can be calming if white predominates. With less white, the room assumes the character of the brighter shade.

It's a question of degree: Do you like your blues intense with almost electric impact, or do you prefer that they offer a cool or subtle seasoning to neutrals? When you examine the blue shades used in each of these bedrooms, you'll find that they're not very different, although they certainly appear to be. The difference lies in how much of the color is used and where.

In the room *above*, walls—the largest surface—are a saturated sapphire as intense as color can be. Soft furnishings repeat this strong color and even intensify it by adding a bold plaid element. The only relief from so much color is a dose of pure white, which appears at the windows and on the bed to balance the impact of the blue.

The lighter room *above* reverses its color priorities and lets white walls and fabric take the lead. When deep blue comes in, it's as part of a small blue and white plaid in which white predominates. Even the carpet is a blend of the two colors, with the blue softened slightly because the floor is such a large area. Most of the decorative impact in this room comes from the unusual pillows, but look closely at the colors. One of these blues is also deep sapphire, in lines so fine that it appears to be a paler shade.

GREEN

Like grass, green pops up when conditions are right. Green mixed with yellow is the color of new plants, promise, rejuvenation, and youth. If leaning toward blue, green is also the color of mature forests, moss on rocks, and seawater as old as time. In your home you can choose to enjoy any shade.

Everything about this slightly offbeat kitchen is family-friendly, including its luscious color scheme. Honeydew green walls and rugs the color of a ripe cantaloupe are an energetic, summery combination, made more appealing by large amounts of white in close proximity.

And which color accents go well with melon and yellow-green? Look toward the warm side of the color wheel and choose analogous colors: deeper tones of orange and green, plus yellows and bits of red—almost any shades of these warm colors work.

Besides color, there's another element that makes the kitchen seem warm—it's the texture of wood. The extraordinary plank-and-beam ceiling, painted off-white so as not to seem too dark and oppressive, adds rugged texture while still reflecting light. Grooved bead-board cabinets echo the ceiling on a smaller scale. The floor is also made of wooden planks, but they're stained honey brown to ground the room. So much off-white and wood provides a clean setting that shows off the brighter colors.

FRIENDLY NEIGHBORHOOD Colors next to each other on the color wheel—yellow and yellow green, for example— always go together. Add interest by including lighter or darker shades of a complementary color.

TOPSY-TURVY If you have a high ceiling, turn the tables on color with a deep-tone ceiling and a much lighter floor. It takes a ceiling higher than 9 feet for this look to work well, but if you have the height, then go for the drama.

If you have a room with a vaulted ceiling, you have a wonderful opportunity to use color overhead. Even though this bedroom is tucked into an area that could have been the attic, generous head space makes up for the fact that side walls are not full height, keeping the room from feeling claustrophobic.

To unify the room's proportions, gentle sage green covers the walls and ceiling, including the exposed beams. A neutral carpet completes the shell, setting the stage for a flowered bedspread with a rich red background.

With a red and green color scheme, why doesn't the room look like a Christmas card? Look at the particular shades—neither the greens nor the red are pure hues. Each has been blended with yellow, resulting in sage greens and a red that is on the rust side. Blended though they might be, these two shades still are complementary, making them a good combination in rooms where you want color excitement but not too much brightness.

Wouldn't it be relaxing to sink into this tub and let the water float your cares away? To create the ultimate bathing environment, walls are the blue-green of a stream in a tropical rainforest. Tranquil green can help free you from stress (and when your mind is free from stress, it's more open to creative thought).

Pay attention to how white and other accent colors enhance the green but don't distract. The glass containers are blue, green, and yellow, all colors analogous to pastel green. Hand-painted tiles have an underwater scene of fish and plants in darker shades of green.

One additional color stands out—notice how the hibiscus red stool stimulates the entire color scheme in bold contrast to the greens. This is the benefit of using complementary colors together.

SURPRISING COLOR COMMENT Rescue an unspirited pastel room by adding the spark of its complementary color in a brighter shade. Keep the accent fairly small; it will have a big impact.

What is the most common color for walls? You guessed it—white, chosen because it "goes with everything." It's true that large amounts of white on walls and ceiling start a room off with a clean slate, but unrelieved white can be boring. Why does this room seem so substantial, even though it's based on white? It's because of accent colors and plenty of texture.

This light-filled room avoids the trap of too little color by mixing white with deep green and rosy red, starting with green molding that artfully defines the room's unusual shape. It also combines a host of fabrics in green and rose tones. Notice the plaid sofa fabric in deep-green and white; the window shades are a compatible stripe.

Now take a closer look at textures. Pillows, scattered like pretty red flowers, prove once again that they are an excellent way to add texture or color (and they're so easy to change if you fall in love with a new fabric). The ottoman has thick moss-fringe, the rag rug combines all the fabric colors in a much nubbier texture, and dark wood adds weightiness to the blend.

IDEAL COMPANIONS Whites and off-whites are a flattering background for almost everything, but these versatile neutrals need the help of either color or texture to make them interesting. If adding color, combine white with brights or darks for the most impact.

SEEMINGLY SEAMLESS The eye craves order and likes repetition in color and pattern. To pull rooms together in a cohesive color scheme, repeat a color from one area to the next. As you get farther away from the source, use smaller amounts of the color or change its shade a little.

You may have heard that adjoining rooms should be the same color. Not always true. But make sure that each room has enough of the same color to lead your eye from one area to the next in an effortless transition.

Color unifies these two distinct rooms—a green living room and a cream dining room—separated by walls and a cased opening. In the dining room *above*, a major piece of art in tones of olive green, cream, and gold is the focal point. A distinctive fabric on the chairs has these shades, plus warm brown.

Turning toward the living room *opposite*, notice how the identical colors appear, but they are in different forms. Here the walls pick up olive green from the art; the rug, upholstery, and trim are off-white; frames are rich gold; and curtains and a pillow are made of the same fabric used in the dining room.

The combination of the two rooms is like a good marriage: It's obvious from all the elements they share that the rooms are a pair, but each can stand alone and make its own decorative statement.

If you're fond of a printed fabric but don't know how to bring its colors into your room, begin by analyzing how the fabric works. Consider the proportion of each color: Which ones are most important? Which ones are only small accents? Try to divide your room in the same manner, using the fabric's main color on walls, ceiling, or floor, its next most important for furniture, and its minor colors as accents. Don't be too concerned with matching colors exactly—just make sure they're in the same general range. A little lighter or darker won't matter.

Notice how this room mimics the colors and proportions in one important fabric—the botanical print at the windows contains off-white, khaki, deep green, gold, and coral. Walls and carpet are easy-to-live-with khaki, a good background color that warms the room without being too bold. The green ceiling also comes from the fabric, and the sofa repeats its tone down at eye level. Pillows in a rainbow of lemon and apricot shades—much softer tints of the gold and coral—soften the all-green sofa. Other furnishings echo the fabric's lighter colors in stripes or low-key prints.

B rown, you might think, is much too dark to use in a room with few windows. Wouldn't it be better to choose a lighter color? Not necessarily—a lot depends on when the room will be used. If your family will usually be in the room at night, then a deep color that looks warm and cozy by lamplight may be the best choice you could make.

In this walkout basement family room, brown teams up with pale yellow, black, and beige. The combination is effective because the buttercup yellow upholstery adds a much-needed sunny element, the black adds dramatic accents, and the mid-tone brown walls disappear in low light to let the other colors star. The neutral beige rug and sofa also stay quietly in the background.

Pale yellow and beige are close enough to do the same things—add light and warmth to a room. Beige and brown are also related; beige is simply brown mixed with yellow and a lot of white. Knowing their relationship will help you understand why this trio goes together so well. They have much in common, and you'll find them to be a very livable combination.

LIGHT AND DARK In choosing colors, consider when you will use the room. Will you enjoy it in the morning with sun coming in the windows or will you usually see it under artificial light? Light is firmly linked to color—you can't adjust one without changing the other.

NEVER BORING Repetition is the key to having a cohesive room. To add interest to a mainly monochromatic color scheme, choose one shape or element to repeat in several forms. Circular shapes repeat in this room.

Somewhere between brown and gray, taupe can be an instant indicator that genteel taste prevails. When it's grounded with black and accented with crisp white, the subtle combination is timeless.

When the room and the furniture have uncluttered lines, as these do, good design comes more easily. But how does color help pull this living room together? It is primarily taupe and browns with black and white accents and bits of rust and blue in the rug. A firm hand with few colors—not too much, not too little—keeps the simple elegance on track.

The key element is the rug, where exuberant medallions align themselves in neat rows to create an orderly phalanx. Inspired by the pattern in the rug, round fixtures throw circles of light onto the ceiling and two upholstered chairs continue its lines with broad swaths of cocoa brown fabric.

Blue is a popular choice for bedrooms because it's said to promote relaxation, but other colors can do the same thing. Keep the blue if you like, but try adding a generous helping of golden brown to lift your bedroom out of its blue mood. Closely related to brown, rust also can draw quiet blue, its complement, out of its shell.

Consider how this bedroom uses color to create a visual "temperature." It combines the warming elements of all-brown walls with bits of gold and rust in the rug, and then adds the cooling touches of blue and creamy white. Together these create a temperate zone that pleasantly surrounds the bed with a shell of soothing color.

an a room in a plain brown wrapper (brown walls, that is)
have much of a personality? Absolutely! If you choose
your accent colors wisely and use only accessories you
love, then you'll feel good about how your brown room looks every
time you walk in the door.

Each of these rooms is a very personal space that reflects its
owner's personality. The somewhat masculine library/office *below*

LIGHTER OR DARKER Attractive rooms usually have a mixture of tones that are close but not exactly the same. A color's value (its lightness or darkness) and intensity (how strong it is) are critical— when these vary, the same color produces entirely different effects.

is rich chocolate brown, filled with books, plants, and comfortable spots to read around the fireplace. With black chairs, tortoiseshell bamboo at the windows, and paprika and cream rugs as accents, there's nothing dull about the colors.

The dressing room *above* has a completely different personality even though it contains many of the same colors. The primary difference is the shades that were chosen. The hand-rubbed walls are a much lighter shade of brown, and the dark wood furniture shows to advantage against an all-white rug. Inspired by colors in the lively abstract artwork, accents are muted blue and white with a touch of persimmon red.

ADAPTABLE COLOR Don't let a color scheme determine your decorating style. If you have a favorite combination, use it with any style of furniture; just adjust the color proportions.

Brown, like other neutrals, goes well with a variety of colors. Try combining brown, beige, or taupe with white and one other accent for a color scheme that fits in well with most decorating styles.

These two bedrooms share this combination—but what a difference. One, *above*, is sweetly old-fashioned with brown only in the linens and in draperies made from three different fabrics (each pattern has some of the accent color, but in slightly different shades). Despite this fancy window treatment, the room has a simple demeanor brought about by plain white walls, small-patterned textiles, and antique furniture and accessories.

Now look at the other bedroom *below*—so different in style—with its walls covered in white squares against a field of dark brown. Aside from the round mirror and lamp, most furnishings hold to angular, contemporary lines. Even the bed, which has no headboard, is somewhat minimal. Chocolate brown and pink reappear in the linens, but the only ornamentation is an embroidered design on the white sheets and stacked pillows. The overall effect of such restraint is a room that is clean, simple, and serene.

Two rooms, two looks, one basic color scheme—so select your style and enjoy your favorite colors—whatever they are!

GRAY

Gray—is it a subtle shadow or a dark plume of smoke against the sky? Is it cool, clinical wire-brushed steel or warm, informal weathered wood? This neutral, far from being a predictable blend of black and white, encompasses a range of shades with many nuances. If you haven't considered building a room around a color scheme of gray, perhaps you haven't explored its rich possibilities.

I f your life is hectic, your bedroom may be the only place where you can go to relax. With good planning, you'll have a calming oasis where you free your mind from intrusive elements and refresh your spirit. A restful color scheme is important to the success of such a room, and gentle gray can help you achieve it.

When white and quiet shades of gray collaborate, the simple combination eliminates a lot of visual clutter and transforms the room into a peaceful refuge. Limiting yourself to one color in shades only a few steps apart also lets other accents make more of an impact. In this white shell of a bedroom, the linens and even the painting are warm-tone monochromatic grays, and their restraint puts more focus on the whimsical bed and classical architecture.

NON-COMPETITIVE SPIRIT Closely related neutrals, such as tones of gray, are an ideal setting for art or other items you wish to feature. In a room with little color, form and texture become more important.

NO PERFECT MATCHES As long as your fabric and paint choices share the same underlying tones, don't worry about whether they match exactly. Often a room is more interesting when you choose a variety of shades that are almost, but not quite, the same.

Taking their cues from the abstract painting, warm gray and black team up in a strong and expressive room. The contemporary black furniture is so dramatic that it almost dominates the color scheme, but the bold painting is the room's focal point.

When using only one neutral color plus black, how do you keep the darker tone from overpowering the lighter one and making the room seem too heavy? The trick is to pay attention to the proportions of each color and how much visual weight each one carries. In this room low-slung black leather chairs and a pedestal television are like dark islands in a sea of flooring that repeats the shade of the wall. So even though gray is the lighter tone, it covers far more actual area than the powerful black, making them roughly equal in visual weight.

So much light gray used with all-black furnishings could create a too-stolid room, but several mid-range gray shades and a little black combine in the painting to offer some middle ground. Bright flowers also attract the eye as relief from the two main colors.

Would you have predicted that a room of neutral gray and white with a single accent color could look as lively and inviting as this one? It's because all of the colors have something in common—they're from the warm side of the color wheel.

Although the walls are creamy white, the larger furniture is taupe, a gray-brown shade with the properties of a neutral as well as of brown. Like other gray neutrals, it's compatible with almost any color, but like brown, it looks best with those that have red or yellow undertones. Bright red is a perfect accent. But how does it affect the room?

The spirited red immediately grabs your attention, adding dynamic motion to the mainly neutral color scheme. It leads your eye from one place to another, hopping with ease from chair to chair, from blanket to pillow to mantel, and then back again. Blonde wood also nudges the room toward informality. Another neutral, black, adds dark emphasis to the art and counteracts the lightness of so much white.

VERSATILE NEUTRAL Taupe is one of those grays that is comfortable dressing up or down. In an upscale room with designer furnishings, it has an air of sophistication. In an informal room that already has a jangle of colors, it creates order and separation without spoiling the fun.

G ray, white, and black—color schemes featuring these classic, no-color neutrals always look good no matter how you vary the individual shades. Do you want a warm room that tolerates the addition of some brighter accents? Then choose off-white and a gray with brown or green undertones. Does your room get so much light that you need to cool it down? Choose pure white and

gray with a slight blue or purple cast. Even black, as dark as it is, leans toward either warm or cool. Decide on the color temperature you want, and choose your shades accordingly.

These two living rooms have basically the same color scheme—warm gray walls, white ceilings, and black, plus pale gold accents—but they part ways when they put the proportional emphasis on different shades. In the room, *left*, extra white in the moldings and two-tone-stripe fabric adds a light and airy quality. In the other, *above*, larger doses of dark color produce a richer, more forceful character. Which is the better choice? There isn't one. Let your own preference be your guide.

ADJUSTABLE SHADES Perhaps you have adjoining rooms and to unify them, you're using one neutral color scheme. You still can emphasize a different shade or use different accents in the two rooms.

With so many attractive towels, shower curtains, and accessories available, painting the bath a neutral color is often the best way to go. White and beige are safe choices, of course, but why not consider gray? This underused neutral is a stylish background for most light or bright colors, and if you choose a compatible gray, it even looks good with dark tones.

This bath has bright white tile and the same white on the ceiling, which is good because reflected light and true color are important in any room where you look in the mirror. But so much white clears the way for a deeper shade on the upper walls, where a hand-rubbed gray-green finish looks almost like pewter. Dark wood and a much paler gray marble floor heighten the elegant effect, but lavender towels add the only other color.

How can you tell if darker walls would be right for your bath? Look at your tile color, the height and color of the ceiling, and also the sources of natural and artificial light. If your room has ample light and reflective surfaces, then tone down your walls with a mid-range neutral shade. If it's not bright enough at certain times, then choose a lighter value of the color.

NEUTRAL PARTY Think in terms of contrast rather than color, and you're likely to make good choices. Medium gray is attractive with jewel-tone accents of sapphire, ruby, emerald, and amethyst. It's also a good background for white or very light shades.

Black and white, those perennial favorites, contradict all apparent logic. According to color theory, black turns out to be a complete absence of color, but pure white light breaks up into every color of the rainbow when it pours through a prism. Regardless of how they come to be, both of these standbys are immensely useful in today's color schemes, providing drama, separation, and extremes of contrast with other shades.

If a color scheme can be said to have a "personality," then this one—composed of black and white plus bright color—is definitely an extrovert. Bold primary hues drawn from a collection of art glass vie for attention against the dark and light opposites. The eye leaps from one color to the next, and the room seems energetic and exciting as a result.

Cool and warm, light and dark, yin and yang—see if you can imagine how this room would look if it didn't have almost equal amounts of soothing white to balance the drama of black, or vice versa. Each holds the other in check, and bright tones provide a continuous dynamic. In color, as in life, balance is vitally important.

THE SQUINT TEST To preview how a new accent color will look in your existing room, prop samples of all colors you're considering against a wall or piece of furniture that you're not changing. With your eyes almost closed, stand back and look at the combination. If a particular shade "pops" much more than the others, you may want to limit it to a small amount or tone it down a little—unless your goal is to add excitement.

Why would anyone want to have black walls? Wouldn't the room look like a cave? Well, yes...and no! Painting the walls black does make them appear to recede, so it's hard to discern the true size of the room, especially at night. But it will also give your room the ambience of an avant-garde gallery where the display of each piece creates maximum impact.

Almost totally unlike in style, these rooms benefit from dramatic black wall treatments. The otherwise traditional dining room *below* departs from the safe path in a big-city approach to color, with all-black walls. This sophisticated room, used mainly at night, has mirror reflections and artificial lights to highlight its pale furnishings, but the walls simply fade into nothingness.

In the more contemporary room *opposite*, a favorite painting seems more important in contrast to its background, an inky black accent wall. The deep-tone wall also fools the eye as to the dimensions of the room, relieving its boxy appearance. You'll notice that in both rooms the ceiling, rug, or trim adds large amounts of white to balance the black and keep the spaces from feeling too dark.

GOING TO EXTREMES Paints and fabrics that first appear to be black or white are actually shades of very dark or extremely light colors. Examine them closely. If you can discern the underlying color family, then follow the guidelines on pages 14–15 to choose accent colors.

CLIMATE CONTROL In a mainly black and white room, accents act like a thermostat to determine the "color temperature." In winter, you can visually turn up the heat with accents from the warm side of the color wheel, or in summer, cool it down with blue-green, blue, or purple.

H ere's another example of using black and white plus color, but this pared-down living room has an entirely different character from the rooms on pages 140–141. It's lively but more focused, perhaps even a bit more intellectual. Notice how the color controls how your eyes perceive the space: Small amounts of black—all below eye level—focus attention downward to ground the furnishings, yet the unbroken whiteness of the walls and ceiling makes the room look larger as well. Instead of multicolor accents that compete with each other, this simpler scheme has only one additional color, a strong and stimulating yellow.

With reflective walls and light pouring in, there's little chance of the space feeling uncomfortably dark. During the day the yellow is only a cheerful departure from classic black and white, but after dark it takes over the job of warming up the room.

To keep an all-white room from looking totally washed out, think about bicycle pedals: When one goes down, the other goes up. It's the same with white: As color goes down, texture must go up. Expanding your palette of textures to include rough and smooth, shiny and dull, and coarse and fine will keep the room calm and simple but never boring.

These two rooms are almost completely white with only traces of color and wood for relief, but look beyond the lack of strong color to see what else they have in common. With nothing to distract, they've focused almost entirely on the interplay of textures. Each has an array of touchable fabrics and trims, a combination of irregular and smooth surfaces, and the effervescent natural froth of flowers—all white, all textural, and all interesting.

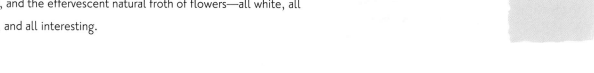

W hite is such a friendly neutral—it goes well with everything. You might also think of white as a bridge between two camps that aren't necessarily compatible. In this children's suite, white is the bridge that separates two rooms with strong pattern on their walls and also unites them.

Baby Girl and Baby Boy have adjoining rooms in what appears to be traditional pink and blue. Look again and you'll see that the colors look pastel only because the drawings on the toile are so delicate—they are actually deeper tones.

Both rooms share one wallpaper in different colors with a white background that ties them together. Lattice on the ceiling is another white element pulling both spaces into one harmonious unit. In each room, a rug echoes the accent color of the paper, but the hallway rug combines both colors, building another bridge.

WHITE WITH BRIGHTS Use white to make an easy transition between two or more dissimilar colors. As long as there is more white than color, the chance of a clash will be minimal.

Adaptable white assumes the character of whatever accent color is used in the room. With other light tints, you'll notice that white seems calm and tranquil. With brighter shades, it becomes more playful. In small rooms such as baths, color possibilities may be dictated by permanent tile and fixtures. It's a plus when these are neutral white or off-white, as they often are in newer houses. Pairing the right wall color and fabrics with adaptable white is usually all it takes to achieve any decorative effect you want.

Older baths often have tiles in unusual colors, but white can help bring them up-to-date. Try teaming old tilework with predominantly white walls and towels. Choose fabrics and accessories that combine white with the tile colors.

HOW DOES LIGHT AFFECT COLOR?

Color and light are so intertwined that it's almost impossible to discuss one without mentioning the other. Every color looks its most pure in natural light coming in through ample windows, but you may have dark rooms with too-small windows. It's practical to consider how colors look under natural and also artificial light in your particular space; otherwise you might be in for a surprise.

When choosing paint and making important purchases, place samples of the color and fabric in the area of the room where they will be applied to see how they look throughout the day. The pale green area rug that is so pretty in the daytime may seem washed out under your kitchen lights, and you may decide that a coral or red rug looks more cozy at night. It's almost impossible to predict which colors are best for certain times of the day

because individual fabric dyes and paint pigments reflect light differently, but you should always try to get a preview.

Consider when you will spend time in the room. Is it primarily in the evening? If so, the type of artificial light you have is especially important. Incandescent light adds a yellowish cast to colors, but halogen bulbs create a whiter, brighter light that may even seem too bright for some tastes. Fluorescent bulbs vary according to which kind they are—warm, cool, and even "daylight" bulbs affect colors differently.

These two rooms have floor-to-ceiling windows that let in an abundance of light. Because they're often used at night for entertaining, they also have multiple sources of artificial light coming from different directions. The high ceilings are painted a warm neutral that recedes at night like a dark sky.

Color palettes are on page 186.

SIMPLE PRECAUTION *Try out as large a sample of the color as you can get, placing it in the area of the room where it will be applied. View it from several angles at different times of the day, with the appropriate lighting, before making a decision.*

CAN COLOR AFFECT THE SENSE OF SPACE?

Traditional wisdom says that light colors recede and dark colors come forward, but this isn't necessarily true. A lot depends on these colors in relation to the light and other colors in the same room. Often it's just the reverse. It's more accurate to say that contrast often determines which colors recede and make the space seem larger. A room in all light colors does appear expansive, but so does a room with all dark furnishings when pools of lamplight make the rest of the room seem to disappear.

Bright spots of color leap forward, while dark spots can either recede or come forward, again depending on the contrast. By understanding how this works, you can use color or neutrals to create dimension where none exists.

This living room, for instance, has cream walls and white trim as the background for neutral furniture. The narrow space between doors had absolutely no focal point—until an enormous framed dark brown canvas created one. Against the light walls, this dark and unexpected contrast begs the eye to search for something in its depths, but the artwork at one corner immediately diverts attention there. Painting only that section of the wall a different color wouldn't have worked, but it gains dimension from the brown—and what a refreshing change from simply hanging a little painting in the middle of the wall! If the framed color block had been a bright color, the entire element would have seemed to come forward, while the dark mat of the smaller painting would have receded.

DEFINING SPACE *Is space only the square footage or the cubic feet in a room? No, it's not. The truest measure of whether space is adequate may be whether you feel comfortable when you're there. Use color to manipulate how the space is perceived—it can make a big difference.*

Color palette is on page 192.

Color palettes are on pages 165 and 186.

SHOULD THE MOLDING
BE A DIFFERENT COLOR?

nless they have texture or a special finish, walls are basically flat, unadorned surfaces. Still they're the largest areas in almost every room, so it is essential that they provide attractive background color for your furnishings.

Moldings are another matter. Sometimes they're so minimal that they are best "painted out" to match the walls. Other times moldings are important decorative elements that deserve the attention a contrasting color can give (see the arched recesses in the room *above*). Determine how much you want to emphasize yours and treat them accordingly.

RULE OF THUMB *If your moldings are wide, unusual, or surround architectural features you'd like to emphasize, paint them a color that contrasts with the walls. If they are nondescript, make them disappear by painting them the same color as the walls.*

You can also enhance the existing moldings if you feel they don't live up to their full potential. You can emphasize them with bright paint that repeats a color used elsewhere in the room, or apply additional moldings alongside the originals for more weight and architectural importance. You can also paint the windows a different color from the window frames (see *pages 74–75*).

Here are some ways to draw attention to the ceiling with moldings and color: Add strips of molding several inches below the crown molding and fill in the space with a special wall treatment, as was done in the room *opposite*. Or attach a frame of molding to the ceiling several inches inside the edge of the room; paint the frame and crown molding a color that contrasts with the wall, and paint the ceiling space between the two moldings a third color.

155

Color palette is on page 192.

HOW CAN I KEEP MY COLORS UP-TO-DATE?

Years pass and fashions change, but some well-dressed rooms never seem to age. They always look attractive, always have interesting accents, and always seem in style. What is the difference between these rooms and those that appear dated? It may be the colors.

Take a look at your own house and you'll see that some furnishings are fairly permanent investments, but others are easier to change. Cabinetry, built-ins, carpeting, wallpaper, elaborate window treatments, sofas, and large pieces of furniture (particularly upholstered pieces or fine antiques) fall into the first category. Painted walls, area rugs, curtains, small chairs and tables, artwork, pillows, and other accessories are not as expensive to change. Let this be a guide to the colors you choose.

Consider adhering to a primarily neutral palette for those items you can't replace easily. Then go as colorful as you like for the other items. If you grow tired of a particular color, then it's easy to introduce change with accessories.

In this living room, for instance, the walls and the large furniture are neutral off-white. Color in the rug is so minimal that it could adapt to other color schemes. Only the smaller chairs have patterned fabric. Vibrant red and green pillows, a painting, and other accessories add bursts of color, yet they could be changed in an instant. The room will remain up to date for a long time if accessories are changed periodically.

COLOR PRIORITIES *Invest in timeless, rather than trendy, big-ticket furnishings, emphasizing neutrals or fairly muted colors. Then choose accessories or less-expensive items in the colors you love.*

HOW CAN COLOR HELP MY ROOMS GO TOGETHER?

used in a conscious manner, color can be the "glue" that holds your house together with harmonious bonds. Or it can be a discordant element that keeps your rooms from looking as though they belong together. It all depends on whether the same or similar colors gently lead your eye from room to room—so choose color schemes that help you keep the peace.

Color is the main factor that makes your rooms look well-planned and cohesive. There must be one or more colors that bridge the gap between adjoining rooms. When these colors appear in both rooms, the repetition draws your eye from one to the other in seamless transition.

Color palettes are on page 165.

Light, bright, dark, and neutral all have their places, but other principles usually determine which you choose.

Examine these two rooms, for instance. Viewing one room from the other is almost unavoidable, but are they the same? No. It's true that they have yellow walls, black accents, white rugs, draperies, and trim in common, but one has pastel accents and the other doesn't. Now look at the two very different bookshelf treatments. In the living room *above*, accessories show best against a background that matches the walls; in the dining room *opposite*, books are displayed against a background so dark that it's almost black. A third room might have this dark color plus a different color, but only slight touches of yellow or white. Color coordination should progress in baby steps, changing slowly from room to room.

NO LOOSE THREADS *As one room leads to the next, color schemes can change as well—as long as any two adjoining rooms have a common thread of color.*

COLOR

SCHEME SAMPLER

The next 32 pages are your color-scheme sampler: Every color palette in the book is reproduced here, large-scale, so that you can cut these pages out and take them with you when you shop for fabric, paint, and accessories. If you like a color scheme you see on the printed page, the best way to reproduce it is to take the page with you as you shop. Match the printed colors to paint chips, or ask the paint store to scan the printed color to determine a matching shade of paint.

The proportion of each color in a palette reflects the amount used in the room shown. You can vary the proportions you use according to your preference, confident that the colors go together well.

Shown on
pages 20–21.

Shown on
pages 26–27.

Shown on
pages 30–31.

Shown on
pages 32–33.

Shown on
pages 34–35.

Shown on
pages 36–37.

Shown on
pages 38–39.

Shown on
page 40.

Shown on
page 41.

Shown on
page 154.

Shown on
pages
158–159.

Shown on
page 7.

Shown on
pages
44–45.

Shown on
pages 46–47.

Shown on
pages 48–49.

Shown on
pages 50–51.

Shown on
pages 52–53.

Shown on
page 54.

Shown on
page 55.

Shown on
page 10.

Shown on
pages 16–17.

Shown on
page 22.

Shown on
page 23.

Shown on
page 23.

Shown on
pages 58–59.

Shown on
page 60.

THE
RED
FAMILY

Shown on
page 61.

Shown on
pages 62–63.

Shown on
pages 64–65.

Shown on
pages 66–67.

Shown on
pages 68–69.

Shown on
pages 72–73.

Shown on
pages 74–75.

Shown on
pages 76–77.

Shown on
pages 78–79.

Shown on
page 80.

Shown on
page 81.

Shown on
page 82.

Shown on
page 83.

Shown on
pages 18–19.

Shown on
pages 86–87.

Shown on
pages 88–89.

THE
BLUE
FAMILY

Shown on
pages 90–91.

Shown on
pages 92–93.

Shown on
pages 94–95.

Shown on
pages 10, 96.

Shown on
page 97.

THE
GREEN
FAMILY

Shown on
pages 24–25.

Shown on
pages 100–101.

Shown on
pages 102–103.

Shown on
pages 104–105.

Shown on
pages 106–107.

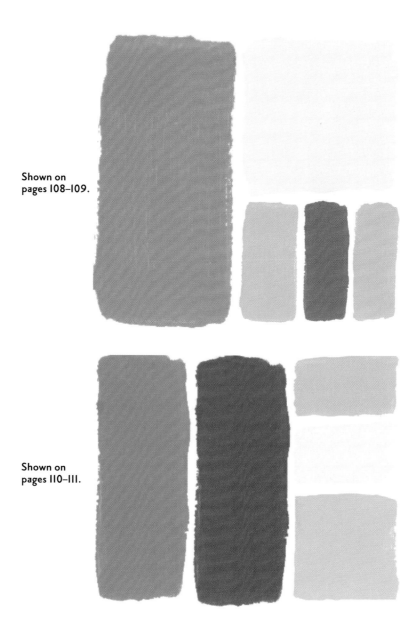

Shown on
pages 108–109.

Shown on
pages 110–111.

Shown on
page 10.

Shown on
pages 114–115.

Shown on
pages 116–117.

THE
BROWN
FAMILY

Shown on
pages 118–119.

Shown on
page 120.

Shown on
page 121.

Shown on
page 122.

Shown on
page 123.

THE
BROWN
FAMILY

Shown on
pages 150—151.

Shown on
page 155.

Shown on
pages 126–127.

Shown on
pages 128–129.

Shown on
pages 130–131.

A RANGE
OF GRAYS

Shown on
page 132.

Shown on
page 133.

Shown on
pages 134–135.

BLACK,
WHITE—
OR **BOTH**

Shown on
page 12.

Shown on
pages 138–139.

Shown on
page 140.

BLACK, WHITE— OR BOTH

Shown on
page 141.

Shown on
pages 142–143.

Shown on
pages 144–145.